BLACK SEA

Corinne J. Naden & Rose Blue

Technical Consultant

Dr. Jacqueline Grebmeier
Graduate Program in Ecology
University of Tennessee-Knoxville

RSVP

RAINTREE STECK-VAUGHN
P U B L I S H E R S
The Steck-Vaughn Company

Austin, Texas

A production of B&B Publishing, Inc.

Editor – Terri Willis
Photo Editor – Margie Benson
Photo Researcher – Ramona Uhlenhake
Computer Specialist – Katy O'Shea
Interior Design – Scott Davis

Raintree Steck-Vaughn Publishing Staff

Project Editor – Helene Resky
Project Manager – Joyce Spicer

LIBRARY OF CONGRESS CATALOGING-IN-PUBLICATION DATA

Naden, Corinne J.
    Black Sea / Corinne J. Naden and Rose Blue.
        p. cm. — (Wonders of the world)
    Includes bibliographical references (p.) and index.
    ISBN 0-8114-6371-0
    1. Black Sea — Juvenile literature. [1. Black Sea.]
I. Blue, Rose. II. Title. III. Series.
GC681.N33 1995
551.46′29 — dc20

94-40912
CIP
AC

Cover photo
Lastochkino Gnezdo, or Swallow's Nest Castle, is an ancient fortress on the Crimean coast.

Title page photo
The Black Sea coast near Sinop, Turkey

Table of Contents page photo
Rumeli Hisari, or the European Fortress, was built by Mehmet the Conqueror in 1452. It is located on the European side of the Bosporus Strait.

PHOTO SOURCES

Cover Photo: © Jan Butchofsky-Houser

© Erik Borset: 20, 37, 39 both, 44, 46 both, 47, 52 bottom, 53, 54, 57
© Ken Buessler: 3, 45 top, 48
© Jan Butchofsky-Houser: 19
© K.R. Downey Photograph: 9, 26 left
Courtesy of German Information Center: 26 bottom
Courtesy of Dr. Jacqueline Grebmeier: 29 right, 30 top, 45 bottom
Dr. Bernward J. Hay: 4, 55
© 1990 B.W. Hoffman: 43
NASA: 21 left, 38
Reuters/Bettmann: 41
Courtesy of the Romanian National Tourist Office: 11, 12 bottom, 13 top, 32 bottom, 33 right, 34, 56 right, 60 right

Courtesy of the Embassy of the Russian Federation: 7, 18 right, 21 right, 22 right, 23 all, 31 middle, 32 top, 35
Courtesy of the Turkish Embassy: 1, 15
Courtesy of the Turkish Tourism Councilor's Office: 10 left, 16 left, 22 left
United Nations 158677/R. Marklin: 42
©1994 Washington Stock Photo/George Petrov: 24, 50
Woods Hole Oceanographic Institution/Richard Harbison: 8 top, 49, 52 top
©WWF/Ernst: 33 left
©WWF/Michel Gunther: 13 bottom
©WWF/Martin Hiller: 5
©WWF/Hartmut Jungius: 17
©WWF/Herve Lethier: 14 left, 56 top, 58–59

Printed and bound in the United States of America.
1 2 3 4 5 6 7 8 9 VH 99 98 97 96 95

Table of Contents

Chapter One

The Sea of Sudden Storms

When adventurer Tim Severin set out to conquer the Black Sea, he took the wisdom of the ancients with him. It was May 1984, and he was retracing the journey made by the legendary Jason and the Argonauts.

According to mythology, Jason and his heroic crew set out in a mighty ship many centuries ago. They crossed the treacherous waters of the Black Sea in search of the prized Golden Fleece. Severin, too, sailed in a ship built by hand, the way the Argonauts constructed their vessel 3,000 years ago. And like Jason, Severin picked only the finest people for his crew.

Retracing Jason's route, Severin and his crew rowed across the Black Sea, past rugged mountains and flat river deltas. They saw wooded countryside on shore, as well as fancy resorts, bustling cities, and huge industrial areas.

However, the modern Argonauts soon discovered the hard truth about rowing a 7-ton ship for 1,500 nautical miles (2,415 km). With ten men rowing at a time while five or six rested, they cut through the sea at approximately 3 knots an hour (3.5 mph or 5.6 kph). The entire journey took three months.

They met their greatest trial when they reached

"Water that pours into the Black Sea can catch ships in eddies and whirl them about like tops."

— Adventurer Tim Severin, after a voyage in Black Sea waters. National Geographic, September 1985

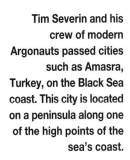

Tim Severin and his crew of modern Argonauts passed cities such as Amasra, Turkey, on the Black Sea coast. This city is located on a peninsula along one of the high points of the sea's coast.

The waters of the Bosporus—the winding strait separating Europe from Asia—may look very calm (above), but the current makes it difficult to navigate.

the Bosporus Strait. This narrow passageway leading to the Mediterranean Sea has a current so fierce that it can whirl ships around like tops. Whitecaps spiked the waters. For every yard the crew advanced in the fierce current, it seemed as if they were pulled back two. At times the ship seemed to spin in the waves. Severin began to wonder if they could make it through the strait.

But slowly, ever so slowly, the modern Argonauts held their ground against the threatening current. After what seemed an eternity, the ship passed through the Bosporus Strait into the calmer waters of the Black Sea. The rowers wearily slumped over their oars.

Tim Severin and his modern Argonauts neither proved nor disproved the wondrous adventures of Jason. But they did establish that centuries ago, a hardy crew could have made that seemingly impossible trip on the unfriendly Black Sea.

Dangerous Waters

The Black Sea was reputed for centuries to be unfriendly to sailors, who called it "the sea of

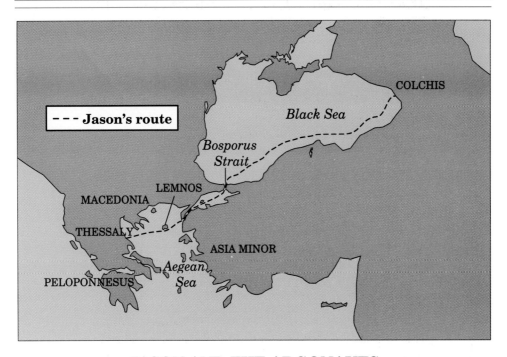

JASON AND THE ARGONAUTS

The often turbulent Black Sea has long been associated with adventure. The challenge of its crossing may have given rise to the Greek myth of Jason and the Golden Fleece. It has become the most famous voyage of legend in the Black Sea region.

The 3,000-year-old epic recounts the Argonauts' perilous adventures as they embarked across the Black Sea with the impossible task of bringing home the Golden Fleece. According to the myth, Jason was the rightful heir to the kingdom of Iolkos in Thessaly (present-day Greece). To gain his kingdom, Jason had to bring back the Golden Fleece from Colchis on the far shore of the Black Sea. Jason recruited the finest seamen for his awesome adventure.

Jason and the Argonauts set out from Thessaly in "the finest of all ships that ever braved the sea with oars." Their first port was Lemnos in the Aegean Sea off Asia Minor (present-day Turkey). From there they sailed toward the Bosporus Strait and the entrance to the Black Sea.

At the entrance to the sea, Jason and his crew met the blind and aged Phineus, who could not eat because his food was constantly spoiled by loathsome winged creatures known as Harpies. After the Argonauts freed him from that bondage, Phineus told them how to pass safely through the treacherous cliffs at the entrance to the Black Sea. These cliffs moved back and forth crushing whatever tried to pass between them. Following the advice of Phineus, Jason sent a dove ahead of the ship, and it passed safely through. After that, the cliffs never closed again.

Jason eventually reached Colchis. With the help of Princess Medea's magic, he overcame many challenges, captured the fleece, and won the heart of Medea.

storms." It was prone to sudden storms, tremendous waves, and strong currents.

For hundreds of years, the Black Sea has been important to the world's commerce. To the ancient Greeks, it seemed the edge of the unknown. For ages, the sea was known by the Roman name Pontus Axeinus, meaning "Unfriendly Sea." After numerous ships survived the crossing, its name was changed to Pontus Euxinus, "Friendly Sea."

After sailors grew familiar with its moods, the Black Sea became a main route for travel and trade between Europe and Asia.

Today, the Black Sea remains an important business and transportation artery, linking southwest Asia and Eastern Europe with world markets. Major port cities line its coasts, and new canals and channels have made the region more navigable for shipping.

People Come to the Sea

The Black Sea and the lands around it are rich in history. For more than 10,000 years, people have lived on its shores. Ancient Greeks and early Turks explored the coastlines of this inland sea and feared the anger of its sudden storms. The Greek historian Herodotus wrote about the Black Sea, its rivers, and the lands that depend on it when he recorded events of an ancient Persian war. During that time, the Black Sea region was the home of peaceful shepherds and fierce warriors.

The first Slavic people settled on the shores of the Black Sea during the Middle Ages. Russian sailors took great pride in their knowledge of the Black Sea, its many moods, and the intricacies of its coastline. They explored the mouths feeding into

The Greek colony of Chersonesus thrived on the northwestern coast of the Black Sea during the 4th and 3rd centuries B.C. Today all that remains are white marble ruins.

Süleymaniye Mosque dominates the skyline on the west bank of the Golden Horn, Istanbul's famous harbor. The mosque was built from 1550 to 1557, during the Golden Age of the Ottoman Empire.

the sea and sought peaceful harbors. They traded heavily with Byzantium, now known as Istanbul, located on the Bosporus. Only Italian sailors showed an equal interest in the Black Sea at that time.

By the 1500s, the Turks of the Ottoman Empire had gained control of the Black Sea. For decades they exercised their power, refusing access to other countries. But finally the Ottoman Empire began to decline, and soon all the countries on the Black Sea had free access to its waters.

What's in a Name?

During the Middle Ages, the sea's name was again changed. It was renamed the Black Sea. This change has prodded centuries of speculation. The water in the sea is not black, so where did the name come from?

Perhaps the Black Sea was named for a dark-skinned people who inhabited the eastern tip long ago. Or perhaps it was named by the ancient Turks who lived along its southern shore. They were so awed by the dark and fearsome storms whipping across the water that they often called it the Karadeniz, or "Black Sea." Some sources suggest the name came from the heavy fogs that still make the sea look threatening today.

The insignia of the Ottoman Empire can still be found at the Grand Bazaar in Istanbul.

A Welcoming Coast

Many people who hear only about its dark, brooding waters imagine the Black Sea as a cold, dreary place. But the Black Sea shore surprises many who think it desolate. In reality, the seacoast is lush and green, with much development and a large population. The people of Eastern Europe flock to the Black Sea to enjoy its mild summertime climate and fine beaches.

Few visitors realize they are swimming in a sea that is 40 million years old. At that time, large areas of Russia were underwater—the Black Sea, the Caspian Sea, and the Aral Sea were one vast body of water. But slowly the Black Sea deepened, and its large basin was formed. As mountains rose around the sea, its links to other bodies of water closed.

Now, the Black Sea's only major links are the rivers that flow into it and the Bosporus Strait leading to the Mediterranean Sea. The rivers bring fresh water, and the Bosporus allows the entry of saline (salty) seawater, making the Black Sea a mixture of both. It is neither fresh like a lake, nor as salty as most seas.

Black Sea Facts

The Black Sea is the world's largest inland body of water. It covers some 162,000 square miles (419,580 km), about the size of Sweden or a little larger than the state of California. Its greatest width from east to west is 715 miles (1,150 km), and its greatest length from north to south is 360 miles (580 km).

Romanian children play at a beach on the Black Sea coast.

The Black Sea is deep, too. About one-third of the Black Sea is more than 6,000 feet (1,800 m) deep, and the basin plunges to 7,200 feet (2,200 m) at its greatest depth.

The total length of the Black Sea coast is about 2,750 miles (4,400 km). If you were to drive a car at an average speed of 55 miles per hour (90 kph) without stopping, it would take you 50 hours to travel completely around the Black Sea. And you

A small village in the mountains near Rize on the Black Sea coast of Turkey

would enjoy magnificent mountain scenery on your journey—except for a few low-lying river deltas.

Six countries border the somewhat oval-shaped sea. Bulgaria and Romania are on its western shores. The newly reestablished nations of Ukraine, Russia, and Georgia—part of the former Soviet Union until 1991—line the Black Sea's northern and eastern edges. Turkey forms the southern shoreline.

Each of these countries has a history as dark and stormy as the Black Sea at its worst. But it is their future that is important to the sea now. Its bordering countries will determine how the Black Sea will be used and how it will be protected. The Black Sea has existed for millions of years. The nations that line its shores can help take care of it for generations to come.

The Black Sea is surrounded by six countries. Four major rivers— the Danube, Dniester, Dnieper, and Don—empty into it.

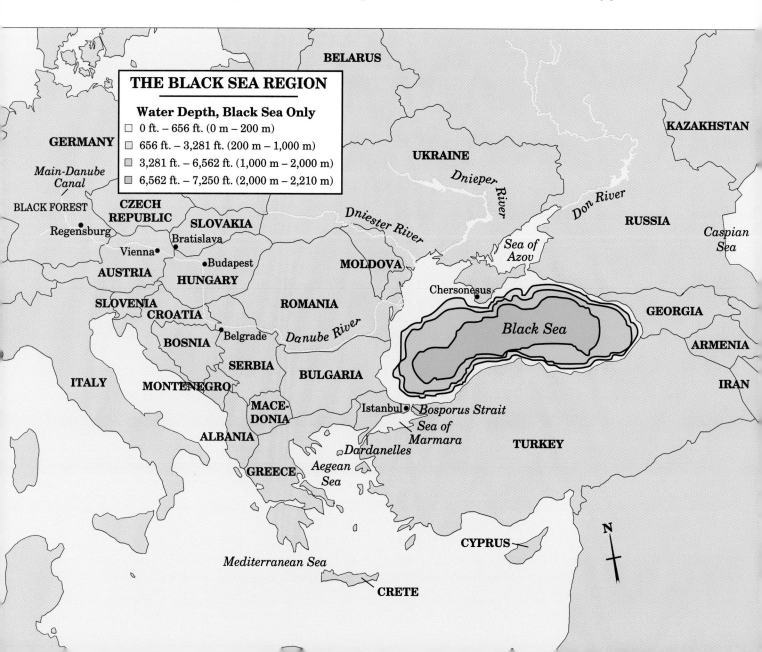

THE BLACK SEA REGION

Water Depth, Black Sea Only
- ☐ 0 ft. – 656 ft. (0 m – 200 m)
- ☐ 656 ft. – 3,281 ft. (200 m – 1,000 m)
- ☐ 3,281 ft. – 6,562 ft. (1,000 m – 2,000 m)
- ☐ 6,562 ft. – 7,250 ft. (2,000 m – 2,210 m)

BELARUS

KAZAKHSTAN

GERMANY

UKRAINE

Dnieper River

Main-Danube Canal

BLACK FOREST

Dniester River

Don River

RUSSIA

CZECH REPUBLIC

Regensburg

SLOVAKIA

Bratislava

Sea of Azov

Caspian Sea

Vienna

Budapest

MOLDOVA

Chersonesus

AUSTRIA

HUNGARY

GEORGIA

SLOVENIA

CROATIA

ROMANIA

Black Sea

ARMENIA

Belgrade

Danube River

BOSNIA

ITALY

MONTENEGRO

SERBIA

BULGARIA

IRAN

MACE-DONIA

Istanbul

Bosporus Strait

ALBANIA

Sea of Marmara

TURKEY

Dardanelles

GREECE

Aegean Sea

CYPRUS

N

Mediterranean Sea

CRETE

Chapter Two

People and the Sea

At least 162 million people live in the Black Sea Basin—the area surrounding the sea, from which all water drains into it. The Black Sea has a tremendous effect on the lives of these people. It provides food, and offers jobs and recreation. But they in turn affect the sea: they can either pollute and destroy it or help preserve it.

Unfortunately, some people who lived in the basin in recent decades have done things that are harmful to the sea. Like many other places around the world, the Black Sea is facing environmental challenges.

To complicate matters, many of the countries surrounding the Black Sea are in turmoil. Serious political upheavals, including the breakup of the former Soviet Union, affected the Black Sea region during the 1990s. Governments are shaky, economies are weak, and leaders are faced with problems that seem far more urgent than environmental concerns. But it's not too late to repair the damage, if people work together.

Romania

Covering nearly 92,000 square miles (238,000 sq km), Romania is a little smaller than the state of Oregon. The capital city of Bucharest, nicknamed the "Little Paris of the East," stands in the southeast on the shores of a northern tributary of the Danube River. Ukraine and Moldova lie to the north and east, Hungary to the west, Serbia to the southwest, and Bulgaria to the south. The beautiful Carpathian Mountains and the historic region of Transylvania are the home of the legendary Count Dracula. Romania's southeastern border runs along the shores of the Black Sea for about 145 miles (234 km). With its mild climate and exquisite sandy beaches, this is Romania's tourist region. Mineral springs dot the area, and many health and tourist centers ring the shores of the Black Sea.

Beautiful beaches and resorts, such as the one above, lie along the 31 miles (50 km) of Black Sea coast south of Constanta, Romania, to the Bulgarian border.

11

Romania is an old land; people have lived in the Carpathian Mountains since 600,000 B.C. When the Romans first ventured to the area they named Dacia, they found a fully developed civilization. Beginning about 300 B.C., the Dacians traded with the ancient Romans, but they were unable to gain control of the Dacians and their lands until A.D. 106. The Dacians were primarily farmers, who had

reached the height of their civilization in the first century B.C., long before the Romans came to conquer them. After the Romans left in 271 A.D., the land was invaded by different people over and over again. Finally in 1859, two principalities, Wallachia and Moldavia, became the nation of Romania.

Romania's King Carol allied himself with Adolf Hitler of Nazi Germany during World War II. His goal was to retain Romania's independence and keep its territory intact. But in 1940, King Carol's plan backfired. Hitler forced the king to give up 40 percent of Romania's territory, containing 50 percent of the nation's people, to Hungary and Bulgaria. Humiliated, the Romanians staged a nationwide protest, and King Carol was forced to abdicate. His son, only 19 years old, became king.

General Ion Antonescu took over the government, and the Romanian armies fought alongside the Germans. However, the Antonescu government was overthrown in 1944, and Romania turned against Germany. Supported by the Soviet Union, the Communists took over in 1947, after World War II. Beginning in the late 1960s, the government was increasingly controlled by Nicolae Ceausescu, whose oppressive regime was finally overthrown in 1989. He and his wife were tried and executed for crimes against the state and its people. Ion Iliescu was elected president, and a new constitution was adopted in 1990.

Most of the great, swampy Danube Delta, where the Danube River meets the Black Sea, is in Romania. Romania's rivers, nearly all of which are

The Danube Delta region is especially beautiful at sunset. More than 80 percent of the delta is in Romania.

The Danube River begins to spread out into a delta near Tulcea, Romania.

Danube tributaries, provide the Danube with nearly 40 percent of the water it discharges into the Black Sea.

Bulgaria

Covering an area of 43,000 square miles (111,000 sq km), Bulgaria is about the size of Tennessee. The capital city of Sofia stands in the west. To the north, Bulgaria shares the Danube with Romania. Serbia and Macedonia lie to the west, Greece and Turkey to the south, and the shores of the Black Sea form the country's eastern boundary.

Like other lands that border the Black Sea, Bulgaria has many picturesque seaside resorts and sandy beaches. However, only a few good ports, such as Varna and Burgas, are situated along this stretch of the coast.

More than 50 percent of Bulgaria consists of meadow, pastureland, and forests. Its main resources come from the rich plains where cereal grains grow and coal is mined. Bulgaria is also home to the mulberry tree, which provides food for silkworms.

Bulgaria's Black Sea coast extends for 153 miles (245 km). There are quiet, untouched beaches (above) as well as busy tourist resorts.

Bulgaria's beginnings date back to prehistory. The country's name comes from the horse-riding Bulgar tribes—Turkish people who lived north of the Black Sea in the 400s.

Like Turkey, Bulgaria was part of the Ottoman

13

Empire for centuries. As the empire declined, the country was increasingly influenced by Russia and Austria. Bulgarian unrest broke out in the April uprising of 1876, which was cruelly and quickly put down. In 1908, King Ferdinand declared Bulgaria independent of the Ottoman Empire. Soon after, Bulgaria became involved in the two Balkan Wars, gaining and then losing large areas of new territory.

At first neutral in World War I, Bulgaria later joined Germany and its allies. After the nation's defeat in World War I, King Ferdinand was forced to abdicate, and his son Boris III ruled until 1943. During World War II, Bulgaria allied itself again with Germany. After the war, however, the Communist party gained control of the government.

Most of Bulgaria's pollution problems are the result of the rush to industrialize that swept over Eastern Europe after World War II. Without safeguards or safe ways to dispose of waste, much of the land and groundwater became contaminated. A marked rise has been reported in such health problems as

The coastal region near Varna, Bulgaria, is quite flat. The famous Golden Sands Resort is located north of this region.

The region near Rize, Turkey (right), is known for its beautiful mountain slopes, lakes, and meadows.

deformed bones and mental illness among Bulgaria's young people. Authorities cannot say for sure that this is the result of pollution, but it seems likely.

Turkey

The Republic of Turkey lies along the southern shores of the Black Sea. The sea coast there is heavily wooded and has a very rainy climate. This part of Turkey is primarily an agricultural region.

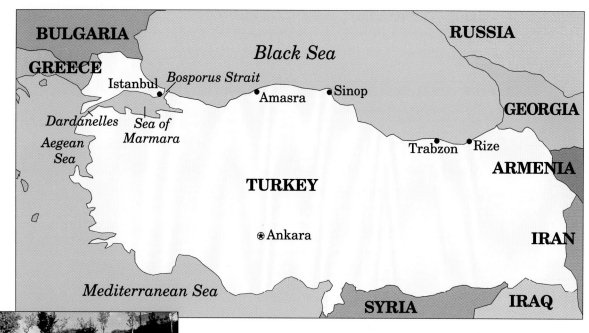

Black Sea

BULGARIA

GREECE

Istanbul *Bosporus Strait*

•Amasra   •Sinop

RUSSIA

GEORGIA

Dardanelles *Sea of*
Aegean   *Marmara*
Sea

Trabzon• •Rize

ARMENIA

TURKEY

⊛Ankara

IRAN

Mediterranean Sea

SYRIA   IRAQ

Workers pick tea leaves at a tea plantation near Rize, Turkey. This mountainous area is known for its delicious blend of Black Sea tea.

Corn is the major crop, and tea is grown along the eastern coastal strip. Copper is mined in the east, and coal in the west.

Besides the Black Sea to the north, Turkey is bordered by Georgia, Armenia, and Iran to the east; Iraq, Syria, and the Mediterranean Sea to the south; and the Aegean Sea, Greece, and Bulgaria to the west. Turkey, the Black Sea's "gateway" to the Western world, lies partly in Eastern Europe and partly in Asia. Its location has deeply affected the nation's history and culture. European Turkey, the western and smaller part, is separated from Asian Turkey, called Anatolia, by the Bosporus and the Sea of Marmara. The capital, Ankara, is in central Anatolia.

Turkey's history also dates back to prehistoric times. Animal engravings on cave walls tell of life long ago in Anatolia. Beginning about 1300, this region became the center of the Ottoman Empire. Osman, for whom the dynasty is named, and his descendants spread the faith of Islam over southeastern Europe, North Africa, and the Arab world. Ottoman rule in Turkey lasted six centuries.

Signs of unrest began to develop in the early 1900s. Turkey lost a huge portion of its territory— the present-day Arab states and Asia Minor—after World War I. The nation fell into civil war and then war with Greece. The present national boundaries were determined at a peace conference in 1923. Turkey then became a republic and began the slow process of modernization under its first president, Kemal Atatürk.

Changing governments marked Turkey's history until 1980 when the military took over. In 1989 Prime Minister Turgut Ozal was elected as the first civilian Turkish president in 30 years. Ozal, with Prime Minister Suleyman Demirel, has worked to establish Turkey as a stable force in a troubled region.

Georgia

This former Soviet republic lies at the eastern end of the Black Sea, with Russia to the north, Azerbaijan to the southeast, and Armenia and Turkey to the south. It covers a small area of 26,900 square miles (69,700 sq km), an area a little larger than West Virginia. The capital city is Tbilisi in east-central Georgia.

Georgia is a land of snow-capped mountains, lush valleys, forests, and rivers. In addition to its famed Black Sea resorts, Georgia is known for its natural resources of manganese, coal, and nonferrous metals.

Mount Usba, rising 15,403 feet (4,695 m) above Mestia, will be part of a new national park in the beautiful central Caucasus Mountains of Georgia.

Georgia's major rivers in the west, the Inguri, Rioni, and Kodori, rush down toward the Black Sea from the Caucasus Mountains. The Kolkhida lowlands on the Black Sea shores are covered with a thick layer of river-borne deposits that have piled up over thousands of years. This area on the Black Sea has a humid, subtropical climate.

Georgia has a long and varied history, with evidence of prehistoric people in the area. It was dominated by the Turks and Persians from the Middle

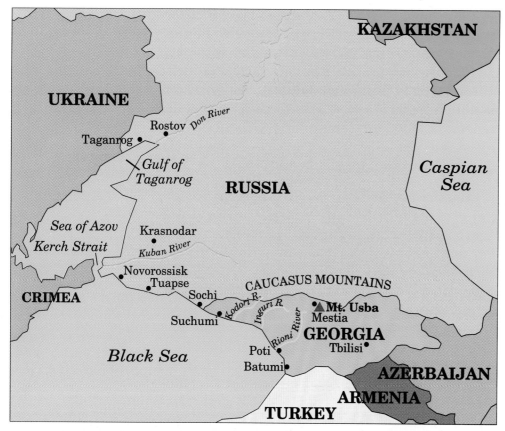

Ages until the mid-1800s. At that time the Russians entered on the scene. But in 1918, the Georgians placed themselves under German protection and declared independence. With the defeat of Germany, the British took over Georgia. The Allied forces recognized Georgian independence in 1920, but in 1921 the Red Army entered the capital city. Georgia was a full member of the U.S.S.R. from 1936 until the Soviet Union broke up in 1991.

In January 1992, the elected Georgian president was overthrown in a bloody battle. That October, former Soviet Foreign Minister Eduard Shevardnadze was elected chairman of the Georgian State Council. Although Russia has recognized Georgia's independence, there is continuing friction between the two former Soviet republics.

Russia

The huge country that is Russia has a small but important access to the waters of the Black Sea. Russia occupies much of eastern and northeastern Europe and all of northern Asia. Its population—over 140 million people—made up more than half that of the former Soviet Union. Even without the rest of the former Soviet republics, Russia is the largest country in the world—more than 6.5 million

Eduard Shevardnadze is now chairman of the Georgian State Council. He served as foreign minister during the last Communist regime of the Soviet Union under Mikhail Gorbachev.

square miles (17 million sq km)—about twice the size of the United States.

Agriculture is important to the Russian economy, and major crops include barley, oats, potatoes, apples, rye, wheat, and sugar beets. Moscow, Russia's capital city, is a major manufacturing region, especially in the production of steel and other metals.

The area of Russia that borders the Black Sea is called the Caucasus. Like other countries that touch this body of water, Russia's Black Sea region is a health and resort area. It boasts a mild climate, warm waters, and mineral springs.

Along with the other republics of the former Soviet Union, Russia suffers from political unrest. Boris Yeltsin is president, but his power is threatened by those who wish to see Russia return to a communist economy.

Ukraine

With 233,000 square miles (603,700 sq km), Ukraine is a little smaller than Texas. Although it covered less than 3 percent of the land in the former Soviet Union, it accounted for 20 percent of Soviet industry. Ukraine also produced 25 percent of Soviet foodstuffs, earning the nickname "breadbasket of the Soviet Union." The former Soviet states of Belarus and Russia border Ukraine on the north and east, the Sea of Azov and the Black Sea lie to the south, Moldova and Romania lie to the southwest, and Poland lies to the west.

These folk dancers are dressed in the traditional costumes worn by people in the region near Yalta, Ukraine.

More than 60 percent of the land is pasture and woodland. Ukraine is also rich in minerals and ore. At one time, it was the Soviet Union's main source of wheat. Unfortunately, it may now be known primarily for the 1986 meltdown in the nuclear reactor plant at Chernobyl—one of the most frightening nuclear accidents in modern history.

One out of three Ukrainians makes a living in shipping or other water-related businesses. The port of Odessa in southwestern Ukraine is the country's busiest Black Sea port, offering access to the world's shipping lanes.

Throughout its history, Ukraine has had many masters. Like Poland, it was used as a doormat for political conquest. In the year 1000, Vladimir the Great ruled a loose confederation of Slavic peoples in eastern Europe, including what is now Ukraine. In 1569, Poland, united with Lithuania, took control of the area.

Less than a century later, peasants known as Cossacks defied Poland and declared their own state. They entered into a pact with Muscovy, now known as Russia. By the late 1800s, most of Ukraine was part of the Russian Empire. After the Russian Revolution of 1917, Ukraine enjoyed a short spurt of independence. That ended in 1920, and Ukraine became a Soviet Socialist Republic in 1922. It has been an independent republic since 1992, but its economy is failing miserably, and many Ukrainians are seeking to realign with Russia.

Yalta is Ukraine's main resort area with many beautiful tourist hotels.

Ships Out on the Sea

The waters of the Black Sea have played a key role in the working lives of the coastal residents. Many jobs and businesses rely heavily on the sea and its resources.

Shipping was a major industry for all the former Soviet nations on the Black Sea coast. More than half the Soviet Union's merchant fleet was registered in Black Sea ports. These ships handled a large portion of Russian oil exports. The main shipping route from the Black Sea through the Bosporus Strait, the Sea of Marmara, the Dardanelles, and into the Mediterranean carried most of the Soviet Union's oil exports.

Shipping continues to be a major industry for countries on the Black Sea. All have large industrial ports, and there is heavy traffic on the water. Ships carry grain, timber, cement, and manganese through the crowded navigation route into the Mediterranean and on out to the rest of the world. About 130 ships pass through the Bosporus on this route each day.

Another boon to shipping has been the 1992 completion of the Main-Danube Canal. This waterway provides a passage from the Danube River off the Black Sea coast northward to the Rhine River, which then empties into the North Sea. From there,

All ship traffic must pass through the Bosporus Strait. This strait looks extremely small as seen from the space shuttle.

Poti, Georgia, is a major shipping port on the eastern end of the Black Sea.

WAR ON THE BLACK SEA

The Soviet Union's Black Sea fleet fought its only major battles during World War II, when confrontations took place on the Black Sea. German troops planned to capture Russian ports using land-based attacks. Though Germany had access to Black Sea waters through an alliance with Romania and Bulgaria, the Romanian and Bulgarian fleets were nearly worthless—only two destroyers and one submarine between the two countries. In contrast, the Soviets' Black Sea fleet at the time consisted of one battleship, 27 destroyers, 6 cruisers, 12 mine-layers, and 50 submarines.

German troops came crashing through Ukraine and into Crimea in 1941, with heavy bombing of the navy's main base in Sevastopol and the important port of Odessa. The Soviet fleet fought back, trying to preserve their ports by bombing the German troops. The Soviets paid a high price, losing many of their destroyers and other ships during the battles. Eventually the remaining destroyers were used only to carry new troops into Sevastopol, which was under heavy air attack by the Germans. However, in July 1942, the Soviets lost control of the base.

A new base was established in Novorossisk, at the eastern end of the Black Sea, but a few months later, the Germans took control of that port, too. Though the Soviets made a few feeble attempts to recapture the base, it wasn't until September 1943 that the Soviet fleet made a strong amphibious landing and was able to take back Novorossisk.

The following spring, the Black Sea fleet made another successful amphibious landing to recapture Kerch, an important port in Crimea. Within a few months, the Soviets swept the Germans out of Crimea and the rest of the Black Sea coast. Romania and Bulgaria surrendered, and by July 1944, the fighting in the Black Sea area was over.

waterways are open to the Atlantic Ocean. Now oceangoing freighters can travel this route, opening a whole new market for goods from the Black Sea region.

Fishing has also played a large role in the Black Sea economy. Thousands of people earned a living from the fertile fishing grounds, catching herring, mackerel, pike, perch, and bream. Fishermen are suffering now, though, because environmental problems in the sea have drastically reduced fish populations.

The Soviet Navy was also a major presence in Black Sea waters. The Soviet Navy established a fleet of ships on the Black Sea in 1918, immediately following the Bolshevik Revolution. The fleet was based in Sevastopol on the Crimean Peninsula, but there were other ports as well, including an important one in Odessa.

Fishing was a major industry on the Black Sea, but this industry has seriously declined.

Because the Bosporus Strait, the only pathway to the open sea, has been controlled by Turkey, the Black Sea fleet has been frustrated by its inability to venture out of the Black Sea. The fleet's only major battles occurred on the Black Sea during World War II.

But the Black Sea isn't just the home of political unrest and war. It has been a peaceful, happy region throughout history as well.

The Red Banner Black Sea Fleet, part of the navy of the former Soviet Union, took part in military maneuvers on the Black Sea. This group is under Russian control today.

Vacation Haven

There are no man-eating sharks in the Black Sea, and no creatures that poison or otherwise harass humans. Swimmers feel buoyant in its salty water, and there are no dangerous tides to worry about. The summertime weather is sunny, the scenery is beautiful, and many of the resorts are luxurious. Most visitors vow to return to this popular vacation spot.

Golden Sands, for example, is the largest resort on the Bulgarian coast. Established in 1956 as the country's first international resort, it now boasts more than 900 bungalows, 80 hotels, and 20 restaurants. Visitors come from all over Europe to enjoy indoor swimming pools, a casino, several nightclubs, and even discos. For those who enjoy outdoor

THE CRIMEA

The Crimean Peninsula, a popular vacation destination, is a large piece of land that juts south from Ukraine, bordering the Sea of Azov to the east. Only the narrow Isthmus of Perekop links the peninsula to the mainland.

From low-lying coastal plains to the north, the peninsula rises gradually to the Crimean Mountains on its southern coast. Dense forests of pine, oak, and beech; grassy meadows dotted with wildflowers; flourishing vineyards; and productive croplands all thrive in the peninsula's rich soil. In addition, the region has large deposits of limestone, marble, and iron.

Crimea has also had a bloody military history, with many Russian soliders buried in its cemeteries (above). The Crimean War took place on the peninsula and in the Black Sea waters. From October 1853 to February 1856, Russian troops fought against British, French, and Turkish forces, mainly over religious differences. Finally, after Austria threatened to join the others in the fight, Russia accepted peace terms.

Following the Russian Revolution of 1917, the British, French, and Turkish alliance controlled Crimea until Soviet troops took over the peninsula in 1921. Control changed hands again during World War II, with Germany occupying it from 1941 to 1944. During the war, Yalta was the site of a historic conference of leaders of Allied forces—Prime Minister Churchill of Great Britain, President Franklin Roosevelt of the United States, and Josef Stalin of the Soviet Union (left).

After the war, the Soviets took control again. Since the breakup of the Soviet Union in 1991, the Crimean Peninsula has been a part of Ukraine.

Despite its turbulent history, Crimea is best known as a vacation spot. Its beauty, mild climate, and mineral springs make it an ideal spot for the many resorts (right) and health centers that line its coasts. For decades, it was a popular vacation destination for wealthy Soviets and other Europeans.

Like the rest of Ukraine today, Crimea is undergoing serious economic hardships. Few Ukrainians can afford to take vacations, and political conflicts keep most Russians away. There is a strong movement in Crimea to reunify with Russia. This would greatly improve the region's economy and its position as a tourist mecca. However, the movement is unlikely to succeed without the support of the rest of Ukraine.

sports, there is horseback riding, tennis, surfing, sailing, and ferry rides on the sea. But Golden Sands offers even more than these modern-day attractions. Vacationers can also experience the old-world charms of Gypsy camps, forests, and country-side pubs nearby.

The Black Sea coast is truly an international resort and tourist center. As economic conditions in much of the region slowly improve, more and more people will be able to afford vacations, and the Black Sea's popularity will become even greater. Recreation and tourism may soon become the most important industry on the coast.

However, in order to develop the tourist industry to its fullest, the seawater and coasts must be clean and safe. Nobody wants to visit a resort on a foul-smelling sea that is littered with refuse and dead fish. Only sparkling water and bright beaches keep the crowds coming back.

Clearly, water is of primary importance in the Black Sea region. The rivers and the sea itself have helped shape the boundaries of the countries in the area. The waterways between the Black Sea and the Mediterranean made trade and cultural exchange possible between vastly different cultures. The economies of all the surrounding countries depend heavily on the environmental health of the Black Sea.

The world-class Golden Sands Resort on Bulgaria's Black Sea coast attracts tourists and much-needed revenue from all over Western Europe.

Chapter Three

Black Sea Biology: A Delicate Balance

There is no other body of water on Earth quite like the Black Sea. Its natural mix of fresh and saline water has produced a delicate balance of marine plants and animals that live together in very unusual conditions. Environmental problems caused by human activity are threatening to upset this balance. To better understand these problems and their solutions, we need to know how the Black Sea ecology works.

The Rivers

The four largest rivers that flow into the Black Sea are the Dnieper, the Danube, the Dniester, and the Don. The greatest of these is the Danube, which provides most of the fresh water that flows into the Black Sea. Along with many smaller rivers, they all converge to replenish the sea. For centuries they have helped to renew its nutrients and freshen the waves that wash up on its beaches.

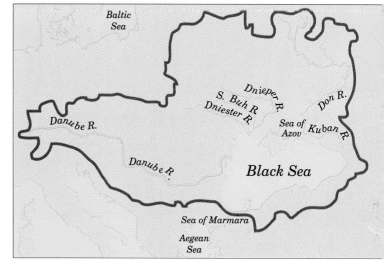

The Black Sea drainage basin covers a region from Germany to Belarus, an area five times bigger than the Black Sea itself.

The Danube flows about 1,770 miles (2,860 km) from its source in the Black Forest of Germany to its mouth on the Black Sea. The Danube begins as a narrow rocky stream flowing northeast. After 200 miles (322 km), it turns southeast into Austria, past the capital city of Vienna. On its long journey, the river is joined by many tributaries that change its width and depth.

The beautiful blue Danube has been celebrated for centuries. In 1867, Johann Strauss the Younger composed a waltz in its honor, making the river a symbol of natural splendor. Today, tourists still cruise slowly down its waters, drawn by the beauty of the villages, farms, and castles that line its shores.

From Austria, the Danube meanders past Bratislava, Slovakia's biggest city on the river. The Danube forms part of the Slovak border with Hungary and divides the Hungarian capital of Budapest. From there, the Danube dips sharply to the south and then east once more as it crosses into Serbia, past the city of Belgrade and across Romania. Beyond Silistra, the Danube swings north and then east, forming most of the border between Romania and Bulgaria and a small part of the border between Romania and Ukraine. Here the Danube's journey ends in a salty delta at the Black Sea.

The Danube is of great economic importance to the countries that touch its shores—Germany, Austria, the Czech Republic, Slovakia, Bulgaria, Hungary, Serbia, Romania, and Ukraine. Most important is the movement of freight through such major ports as Regensburg in Germany, Ruse in Bulgaria, and Izmail in the Ukraine delta. The waters of the Danube also generate hydroelectricity and are important to irrigation and the fishing industry. With the Main-Danube Canal, the river provides a water link from the North Sea to the Black Sea.

The Dnieper is Europe's fourth longest river, after the Volga, Danube, and Ural. It begins near Moscow in Russia, flows generally southward for 1,367 miles (2,199 km), and enters the Black Sea near Kherson, Ukraine.

In modern times, the river was under Soviet control, and the first hydroelectric plant was completed in 1932. Dams and dredging diverted the

The Danube River runs past gently rolling hills in Romania before reaching its delta.

The Danube River flows past Walhalla—home of Ludwig I from 1830 to 1842—near Regensburg, Germany. The elevation of the Danube is at its highest point at Regensburg.

river's waters through the years and changed its ecology. Industrial waste in the 1900s has polluted the waters. Wetlands around the Dnieper have been seriously damaged, and about 20 percent less water from the river now reaches the Black Sea.

The Dniester River, 840 miles (1,352 km) long, empties into the Black Sea near Odessa, Ukraine. It originates in the Carpathian Mountains and picks up many tributaries on its way. However, only 15 of them are more than 60 miles (97 km) long. Although navigation is difficult in the lower section because of shallow water, the river is used extensively for floating logs down to the Black Sea.

One of the great rivers of what was once the Soviet Union is the Don. It is 1,162 miles (1,871 km) long, begins south of Moscow, and flows southward where it empties into the Sea of Azov, which is really a large bay on the northern shore of the Black Sea. In the 1900s, the newly industrialized Soviet Union overused the resources of the Don. Dredging to improve navigation and diverting the water for irrigation seriously reduced the flow of the river.

Water Circulation

The Black Sea also has an interesting relationship with the Mediterranean Sea, through the Bosporus Strait. A rapid current carries water out of the Black Sea through the 19-mile (30-km) strait and flows into the Sea of Marmara at the other end of the Bosporus. From there, it flows into a short, narrow strait called the Dardanelles. The Black Sea water then enters the Aegean Sea and flows into the Mediterranean.

However, beneath the outgoing current from the Black Sea through the Bosporus, a strong undercurrent carries salt water in the opposite direction—into the Black Sea. These opposing currents result in the choppy waters that have challenged sailors for centuries, and they have also worked to create a unique environment in the Black Sea.

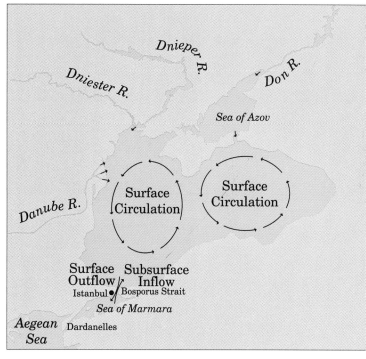

A strong undercurrent brings salt water from the Aegean Sea, an arm of the Mediterranean, into the Black Sea. A surface current carries water out of the Black Sea toward the Aegean.

The Layered Sea

The water in the Black Sea is unusual because of its distinct layering. Though most bodies of water have some differences between their upper and lower layers, none are so markedly different as those of the Black Sea. In the upper layers, plants and animals thrive, but in layers below 328 feet (100 m), there is a dead zone, almost totally devoid of life.

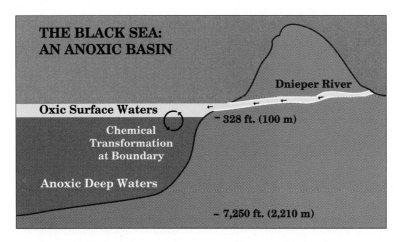

THE BLACK SEA: AN ANOXIC BASIN

Dnieper River

Oxic Surface Waters

– 328 ft. (100 m)

Chemical Transformation at Boundary

Anoxic Deep Waters

– 7,250 ft. (2,210 m)

The bottom anoxic layer of the Black Sea is virtually "sealed off" from the top water layer. Some elements, such as sulfur, chemically change at the boundary between the oxic and anoxic waters. Sulfur is reduced to hydrogen sulfide, a gas that smells like rotten eggs.

The huge bottom layer is anoxic, which means that there is no oxygen dissolved in the water. Only a few specially-adapted forms of bacteria can live in such conditions. Nearly 90 percent of the Black Sea is anoxic—it is the largest mass of anoxic water in the world.

This layering is a result of the way water enters the Black Sea. Because nearly all of the sea's fresh water enters from rivers, it flows into the shallow coastal areas of the sea. But as the salt water enters from the undercurrents through the Bosporus Strait, it flows into a deeper level. And because it is denser, the salt water continues to sink, filling the deepest layers first. Therefore, the lower layer of the Black Sea is far more saline than the upper layer—about 23 parts per thousand saline in the lower layer, compared with 16 parts per thousand in the upper layer.

The water on top is, in a sense, "floating" on the saltier, denser lower layer. Because of this, the upper and lower layers mix very little. Any mixing usually takes place from 165 feet to 245 feet (50 to 75 m), with salinity increasing rapidly between 200 feet and 235 feet (60 m to 70 m). Because of this lack of motion and mixing, scientists estimate it would take about 2,500 years for the sea's water to completely renew itself below 100 feet (30 m).

The Dead Zone

When marine life—plants and animals—die, they settle to the bottom of the sea. As they decompose, they use up oxygen. At the bottom of the Black Sea, most of the oxygen has been used up in this way. The only oxygen in the water is the small amount contained in the salt water entering through the Bosporus. It is quickly used up, leaving the water without dissolved oxygen. The lack of mixing between the layers is what causes the lower layers to be anoxic.

But the lower level is rich in another sort of gas—hydrogen sulfide, a form of sulfur that occurs where oxygen is absent. Most of us are familiar with the nauseating odor of hydrogen sulfide— it smells like rotten eggs. And that's exactly what the Black Sea's deep water smells like.

Oceanographers collect water and sediment samples from the Black Sea to learn about the conditions deep below.

Many oceanographers are intrigued by the Black Sea because of the extreme conditions that exist in its lower level. Many interesting chemical reactions take place at the border between the oxic and anoxic water. Scientists have learned a great deal by doing experiments there. But they must get used to the sickening hydrogen sulfide odor quickly. Any instruments lowered into the anoxic zone come up with metal stained black from the sulfur—and they smell awful!

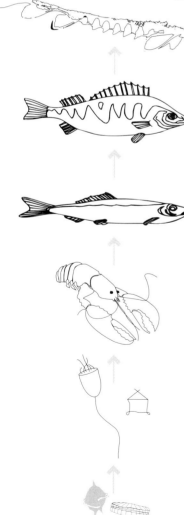

Small microscopic plants called plankton are at the bottom of the food chain in the Black Sea. Small invertebrates, crustaceans, and fish are in the middle. And large fish, such as sturgeon, may be at the top.

Life on Top

Though the Black Sea's lower levels may be dead and malodorous, a bountiful layer of water rich in marine life lies on top. Because the water is a mix of saline water and fresh water, the Black Sea provides a habitat for many marine species not found in other seas or lakes.

The base of the food web in the Black Sea, as in most bodies of water, consists of microscopic plants called plankton. The food web is the chain of life in a community—linking the smallest plants and animals to the largest. Usually, the large feed off the

small, and energy is transmitted up the web as nutrients. Plants are always at the base of the food web because they manufacture their own food using energy from sunlight to perform photosynthesis.

In the Black Sea, 334 types of bacterial plankton, which are microscopic marine plants, form the base of the food web. Phytoplankton, another kind of microscopic marine plant, is also at the base of the food web, but there is far more bacterial plankton in the Black Sea.

Zooplankton are tiny, sometimes microscopic, animals that feed off the bacterial plankton and phytoplankton. There are nearly 100 species of zooplankton, including the larvae of shellfish and other larger animals.

Next in the food web are mollusks, animals such as clams and snails. A few Black Sea varieties are very abundant and popular with gourmets around the world—and these have been fished heavily. Mollusks eat a variety of microorganisms and loose organic material. Some species eat protozoa, algae, crustaceans, or other smaller mollusks.

Some of the larger plants in the Black Sea are seaweeds. These 300 species of green, red, and brown algae live in the upper layer of the sea, from the surface to a depth of 65 feet (20 m). These plants are also part of the base of the food web and are eaten in turn by animals such as large fish.

The top of the food web is made up of 165 types of fish. Commercial fishers catch about 15 species,

Coccolithophorides (top), dinoflagellates (left), and diatoms (right) are types of plankton that grow in the Black Sea. Coccolithophorides are nanoplankton, the smallest of all plankton species. Although they are very common, these plankton have very little food value.

The surface waters of the Black Sea are somewhat salty—about half as salty as the ocean. This oxygenated surface layer is full of life, ranging from tiny plankton to many species of fish.

particularly small anchovies. Anchovies, which feed on plankton, are the most abundant fish in the Black Sea. The second most numerous are the Mediterranean horse mackerel, along with its close relative, the Atlantic horse mackerel. These fish eat zooplankton and small fish.

The bluefish migrate from the Mediterranean Sea to the Black Sea in the summer, where it feeds on anchovies and mackerel, and produces its young. In the autumn, schools of bluefish migrate back to the Sea of Marmara and on into the Mediterranean.

The turbot has great commercial value, but so many have been taken from the sea that they are becoming rare. Turbot spawn in the spring, and feed on small fish, shellfish, and clams.

Four different kinds of sturgeon live in the Black Sea region, two in the rivers that feed the sea, and two in the sea itself. Sturgeon are valued not only for their flesh, a source of food, but also for their eggs and their swim bladders. The eggs are sold as a delicacy, called caviar. The swim bladders are used to make isinglass, a transparent, almost pure gelatin.

The two river sturgeon are the *Acipenser guldenstadtii* and the *Acipenser stellatus*, which has a very recognizable pointed snout. The two sturgeon species found in the Black Sea itself are the *Acipenser ruthenus* and the *Acipenser huso*. The *ruthenus* is valuable as a food fish and averages 3 feet (0.9 m) in length. The *huso*, by comparison, can reach 10 feet (3 m) in length and weigh about 1,100 pounds (500 kg), but because of overfishing and poaching, catching a fish of this size is very rare. This larger fish is a less valuable catch than its smaller relatives.

The spiny dogfish is found throughout the Black

Many of the countries surrounding the Black Sea used to rely on its waters for fish. Catches from all countries surrounding the Black Sea have fallen from 900,000 tons (816,480 mt) in 1986 to 100,000 tons (90,720 mt) in 1992.

Four kinds of sturgeon live in the Black Sea region and the rivers that flow into it. Russian scientists recently detected high levels of pesticides, such as DDT, in sturgeon and other fish caught in the Don River and in the Gulf of Taganrog.

Some countries surrounding the Black Sea have set aside marine reserves, such as the Sukhumi Dolphin Aquarium in Georgia (right), to protect Black Sea dolphins.

Sea, traveling in schools. It eats various fish and shellfish, including clams.

The largest mammals in the Black Sea are three species of dolphins, the top predators in the food web. They usually gather in schools and consume such fish as anchovies, horse mackerel, and bluefish. At one time, more than a million dolphins lived in the Black Sea. There are no recent estimates about the dolphin population, but they have been seriously depleted by commercial fishing and are now protected.

Wildlife on the Coasts

The upper layers of the Black Sea are not, of course, the only places where life flourishes. Wildlife also abounds along the Black Sea shores.

The diversity of landscape in the Black Sea region provides habitats for a wide variety of animals, plants, and fish. The thick forests covering the slopes of the Transylvanian and Carpathian mountains provide shelter for mountain goats, foxes, and bears, as well as eagles and bats. For centuries, Russia's flat treeless grasslands, or steppes, have provided grazing for cattle and sheep, and open spaces for raising chickens and breeding horses. The steppes are also home to rodents such as the marmot, jerboa, and hamster; birds like the kestrel, crane, eagle, and lark; and predators, including the masked polecat and the Tartar fox.

The rugged Carpathian Mountains of east central Europe provide habitat for numerous animals. Runoff water from this area also empties into the Dneister and Danube rivers as they flow toward the Black Sea.

The Danube Delta

Perhaps the greatest concentration of life on the shores of the Black Sea is found in the Danube Delta. Here the Danube River divides into three main branches that flow into the Black Sea. A patch of land has formed between each of these channels as a result of the buildup of soil and debris washed down the Danube over centuries.

The Danube Delta covers an area of some 2,000 square miles (5,180 sq km)—about the size of the state of Delaware. Like other deltas, the Danube Delta is roughly triangular. The continuous buildup of mud and silt makes the soil of the delta rich and fertile. With more than 25 types of natural ecosytems, it is no wonder that over 1,100 species of plants, including the largest area of reeds in the world, grow in this region.

The Danube Delta has areas of thick vegetation. Vines often hang from the branches of oak, willow, and poplar trees, and many flowering plants add color to the greenery.

Sand dunes and grasslands, forests and marshes, river channels and lakes make this one of the most important wildlife areas in Europe. The Danube Delta is a stop along the migration routes of more than 300 types of birds, and more than 200 species breed there. They come from Africa, Asia, and even beyond the Arctic Circle.

Beautiful insects, such as the Apollo butterfly (above), are plentiful in the Danube Delta as are fish and mammals.

About half of the world's pygmy cormorants and white pelicans make their homes in the delta, along with spoonbills, mute swans, great white herons, and rare white-tailed eagles. More than a million ducks, geese, and other waterfowl take refuge in the delta during the winter months.

Other residents include mammals, such as boars, otters, minks, and ermines. The reed wolf makes its home in the delta, living, as its name suggests, among the small, floating reed islets there. It feeds on rodents, birds, and larger animals that are weak or injured.

Regular delta floods are a natural phenomenon, so most animals have adapted to cope with the water. Some, like the reed fox, live on floating islets, while others build nests high in trees. Still others, such as wolves, simply head for higher ground during floods.

Trouble for the Delta

But the greatest hardship facing the animals of the Danube Delta is not due to flooding. It is the result of human activity.

In the 1970s, Romania's leader, Nicolae Ceausescu, wanted to use every bit of the land to build the economy. Intensive forestry, fishing, and agricultural projects were started in the Danube Delta.

As a result, trees were cut down, and several fish populations were seriously depleted. Water was drained from its natural delta location and used elsewhere for farming. Some delta marshes were drained for use as cropland. Runoff from farming polluted what was left of the delta with pesticides and fertilizers. Many plants and animals died.

Today, international environmental groups are working together to save the delta. Among their projects is an effort to return about 75,000 acres (30,000 ha) of abandoned farmland to its natural condition. But any major efforts to undo the damage to the delta will probably have to wait until Romania's economic situation improves.

The new Romanian government is also taking steps to protect the delta. In 1990, the Danube Delta Biosphere Reserve was created. It preserves much of the remaining, healthy delta areas, which provide resting places for migrating birds. Unfortunately, this protected area is only about one-tenth of the entire delta, and the rest of the area continues to deteriorate.

The problems facing the Danube Delta reflect the problems faced by the entire Black Sea region. People have tampered with the ecological balance, and now the disastrous results are coming to light.

PELICANS ON THE DANUBE DELTA

In the past, many thousands of birds known as white pelicans made their homes in the Danube Delta. These large birds have lovely pink feathers. They carry their meals of fish in pouches that hang from their bills. Their habitat used to be a noisy center of pelican activity.

Now the bird sounds are gone, replaced by the noise of machines such as tractors, harvesting tools, and motorboats. The changes in the Danube Delta have had a particularly hard impact on pelicans. They have served as a sort of "ecological barometer" over the last few decades in their reaction to the changes in their living conditions. The disappearance of pelicans reflects the area's troubled past and hints at problems to come.

For example, pelicans typically feed on the weakest fish in the delta. In doing so, they help, by selection, to strengthen the fish population. With the pelican population being depleted, fish diseases spread rapidly, beginning with the weaker fish. As a result, the entire fish population is being destroyed.

Chapter Four

Troubled Waters

"From the Baltic to the Black Sea, half a century of runaway industrialization has left a smear of destruction through the heart of Eastern Europe."

— **Jon Thompson,**
National Geographic,
June 1991

Many problems facing the Black Sea stem from things people do on the land surrounding it. They divert river water by building dams and dump poisons on the ground that eventually drain into the sea. Some experts claim the Black Sea is more threatened by land-based pollution than any other sea in the world.

Why are people abusing something so vital to their lives? Many times, they don't understand the consequences of their actions.

Consider diversion projects, for example, in which river water is diverted away from the river and used for other purposes. The Black Sea and the rivers flowing into it contain a great deal of water. It doesn't seem harmful to reduce the water level slightly, especially if the water is used for a good cause like growing crops or creating electricity. The problems begin when there are many diversion projects and the water flow is seriously reduced. Unfortunately, this has happened in the Black Sea region.

The Inguri Dam is a large hydroelectric plant built on the Inguri River in Russia. The picture shows the dam's powerhouse.

Diversion Disasters

Most of the diversion projects started after World War II, when the Soviets began water management projects. Large dams were built on rivers that flow into the Black Sea, including the Danube and its tributaries. Water backs up behind these dams, forming reservoirs that help produce hydroelectric power.

At the same time, the population increased around the Black Sea, creating a greater need for municipal water supplies. And, of course, more people need more food, so agricultural production has also increased, creating a greater need for water to irrigate crops.

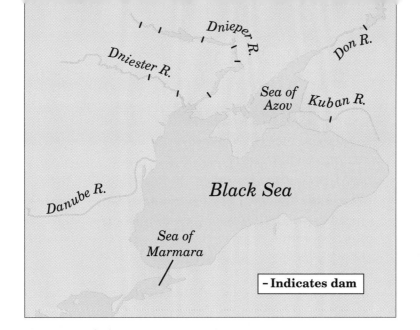

The map shows hydro-electric plants and water storage reservoirs on the major rivers emptying into the Black Sea. Construction of dams has made navigation easier on the Don River for about 1,300 miles (2,100 km). It has also drastically cut the amount of fresh water reaching the Black Sea.

Several rivers draining into the Black Sea have been reduced by as much as 50 percent, and the total amount of river water flowing into the Black Sea has been reduced by about 15 percent, with an even greater reduction predicted for the future. Of course, when less fresh water comes into the Black Sea from rivers, more comes in from the Mediterranean to make up the difference. The overall level of the water doesn't fluctuate very much. But because river water is fresh water, and Mediterranean water is salt water, the unusual water composition of the Black Sea is changing. This could have very serious implications for the survival of the living things in and around the sea.

REDUCTION OF WATER FLOW INTO THE BLACK SEA
(% Reduction)

River	1971-1975	1981-1985	1991-2000 (projected)
Don	19%	27%	43%
Kuban	39%	49%	65%
Dnieper	24%	52%	71%
Dniester	20%	40%	62%

Oceanographers are concerned about the reduction of river water flowing into the Black Sea for several reasons. One problem is that the sea's surface water is becoming more saline, because more salt water is now flowing in from the Mediterranean.

As the Black Sea's surface water becomes more saline, greater mixing could occur between the upper and lower water layers, because their density will become more even. This could have disastrous effects. If the anoxic water on the bottom, rich in hydrogen sulfide, mixes with the surface water in which life forms exist, many plants and animals could be killed off.

The first hints of such a possibility now exist. Scientists report that sulfide has risen to a higher level, and there is a thin zone between the oxic and anoxic zone—the suboxic zone, with both low oxygen and hydrogen sulfide.

Fish have changed their migratory patterns because of the changes in the water makeup of the Black Sea, adding to the problems faced by fishermen. Several types of fish now have much smaller populations, including the valuable sturgeon.

Pollution Problems

Like many other rivers in the world today, the rivers that flow into the Black Sea are often seriously polluted. How did things get so bad for so many waterways in Eastern Europe? The problem really began after World War II. The Communist government of the Soviet Union was intent on modernizing the country in a hurry. Many Eastern European leaders tried to follow the Russian methods. But they lacked the natural, political, or economic resources to do so.

Industry and government managers knew little about—and paid less attention to—treating wastewater or to disposing of solid wastes. Untreated wastes seeped into the ground and contaminated not only the land but also the groundwater. Many cities and plants along the shores of the Danube River and other Eastern European rivers still dump untreated waste into the waters.

Bulgaria provides a vivid example of the drastic effect human activity can have on a body of water such as the Black Sea. Bulgaria's river water comes from tributaries of the Danube. About 85 percent of this water is heavily polluted by industrial waste. And more than half of the runoff from this polluted water drains right into the Black Sea.

Among the pollutants are large quantities of nutrients, called fertilizers, washed away from farms. An excess of nutrients may not sound too harmful, but they seriously disrupt the food web.

Hazardous chemicals in the untreated wastewater from a Romanian chemical plant flow into streams and rivers that eventually empty into the Black Sea.

37

Effects on the Food Web

The northwestern shelf of the Black Sea is facing a critical problem. Most of the sea's plants and animals live there. And most of the rivers enter the Black Sea there, carrying pollutants with them. So the contamination enters exactly where it can do the most harm.

In a process called eutrophication, huge amounts of minerals and organic nutrients in the water make it easier for plant life to grow, while animal life suffers. This process depletes the supply of oxygen in the water. Most of the minerals and organic nutrients enter the northwestern shelf by way of the Danube, as well as from other rivers that spill into the sea. The Danube River deposits about 60,000 tons of phosphorus per year and about 340,000 tons of inorganic nitrogen. Phosphorus and nitrogen are nutrients—chemicals that help plants grow.

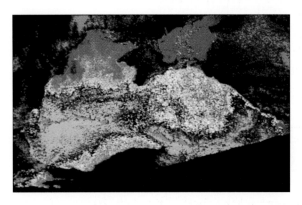

The bright red in the Black Sea picture above—obtained by NASA's Coastal Zone Color Scanner—depicts a high concentration of nutrients flowing into the sea from the major rivers.

In the past 25 years, the amounts of phosphorus and nitrogen entering the Black Sea have risen tremendously for two major reasons. First, the use of phosphate detergents is growing in the Black Sea region. When wastewater containing these detergents enters waterways, it adds to the phosphorus content. The second reason is the great need for food products in the region. To meet the demand for more crops, farmers are using large amounts of fertilizers containing nitrogen. Also, some communities on the seacoast dump their industrial wastes and sewage—more minerals and organic nutrients—directly into the sea.

A Blooming Dilemma

The addition of organic and inorganic nutrients to the seawater causes increased phytoplankton blooms. Phytoplankton are microscopic floating plants, and they are especially numerous on the shallow northwestern continental shelf. Though the phytoplankton is a necessary source of food for marine animal life low on the food chain, excess amounts of these microorganisms will cause great harm to the sea over the long term.

First, all these new plants must eventually die, and more plant growth results in more dead matter sinking to the bottom of the sea. As it decays, organic matter uses oxygen, and so the amount of oxygen dissolved in the water is further decreased. New anoxic zones are being created, apart from the permanent anoxic layer. Fish that once lived in these zones have died, and fisheries all along the Black Sea coast have suffered tremendous losses.

Secondly, additional phytoplankton blocks the light passing through the water. Light is necessary for most marine life plants to produce food through photosynthesis. The surface layer through which light can pass is called the euphotic zone. The euphotic zone is getting shallower in many parts of the Black Sea. Even in the open waters of the sea, where the euphotic zone was once 164 to 197 feet (50 to 60 m) in the early 1960s, light now reaches down only about 115 feet (35 m). The euphotic zone is less than 33 feet deep (10 m) in some coastal areas. This means that the layer of the sea in which plant life can receive the light it needs to survive is shrinking drastically.

One result of the shallower euphotic zone is that there are fewer macrophytes. Larger than phytoplankton, macrophytes are marine plants that can be seen with the naked eye. Macrophytes were once an important part of the food web in the Black Sea, but few are left today, in some places less than 5 percent of the original population.

Now, instead of macrophytes, nanoplankton grow readily. Nanoplankton are microscopic plant and animal organisms, the smallest of all plankton, with very little food value for animals higher up the food chain. This causes starvation, illness, and eventually death among the larger animals, so other species are able to take over. The Black Sea is losing its great diversity of species.

Waste from a coal-fired power plant is discharged directly into the Black Sea.

Some Black Sea coastal water has become discolored by raw sludge discharged directly into the water without being treated.

Opportunistic Animals

The loss of diversity among animals makes it easy for "opportunistic settler species" to find a niche in the waters of the Black Sea. These species are brought in from other parts of the world, usually in the ballast water of ships. The natural predators of their native environment usually do not exist in their new homes, so they grow unchecked, often with harmful effects on the new environment.

The predatory sea snail *Rapana thomasiana* was the first documented opportunistic settler species in the Black Sea. It arrived in the late 1940s, probably on a Japanese ship, and wiped out the oyster populations, which had been an important economic resource. Other animal species were also diminished. However, in recent years, the sea snail itself has been fished for export to Japan, and its numbers are finally decreasing.

Though there have been other opportunistic settlers in the Black Sea since the sea snail, none have been as threatening as the *Mnemiopsis leidyi*. This undesirable alien has almost taken over the sea.

Mnemiopsis leidyi are ctenophores—small marine animals that look like jellyfish. Their transparent bodies have eight rows of comblike cilia, or hairs, that propel them through the water. They were carried to the Black Sea from the eastern coast of the United States in 1988, and immediately their numbers exploded. The water conditions in the Black Sea are perfect for *Mnemiopsis leidyi*, and they have no natural predators.

Mnemiopsis leidyi feed on a wide range of Black Sea plankton, using up food that other marine animals need to survive. However, they have little food value themselves, so they add nothing to the food web—they only take from it. Because of their demands on the food chain, many fish are starving.

The problems of opportunistic settlers can be overcome, usually by bringing in a species that preys on them. Researchers are now seeking a marine animal that will feed on *Mnemiopsis leidyi* and wipe it out without causing further problems for the Black Sea.

But even if they are successful, there is more to worry about. Researchers must also find ways to get rid of the harmful pollutants that enter the Black Sea and present yet another threat to marine life.

Mnemiopsis leidyi is a colorful ctenophore or comb jellyfish. Called the "colorful killer," the *Mnemiopsis* lights up with beautiful colors when disturbed.

The oil tanker *Nassia* burst into flames in the Bosporus Strait in March 1994 after being hit by a Russian cargo ship.

Chapter Five

Dirty Water

The Cypriot oil tanker *Nassia* ran aground and burst into flames after it was was rammed by a Russian cargo vessel in the Bosporus Strait on March 14, 1994. One crewman was killed, and 15 people were injured, but the response to the oil spill was quick. The strait was immediately closed down, and booms were put in place to contain the oil. Dutch firefighters and pollution control experts arrived quickly to help clean up the oil.

What could have been a major disaster was kept minor because of efficient action. The pollution was kept in check, and that's good. But what's bad is that every day, tons of pollutants enter the Black Sea without being stopped. The pollutants enter quietly. They flow in with the rivers. They seep in from the ground. They don't present an immediate crisis, so they don't draw as much attention as a tanker collision. Perhaps they should.

Rivers of Filth

Nearly all the rivers flowing into the Black Sea are polluted. The Danube in particular is in serious danger. And the Danube provides most of the Black Sea's fresh water.

Today, the celebrated waters of the Danube are often more gray than blue. In some sections of the river, swimming is prohibited because the water is so polluted. Fishermen complain that their catch has an oily taste. Once-rich fishing grounds are depleted, and the river water has become unfit to drink—or even to irrigate crops in many places.

The once-beautiful blue Danube has survived centuries of warfare and destruction, tourist invasions, and great industrial growth. Now, worried environmentalists wonder if it can survive what is perhaps its worst enemy—pollution in the late 1900s. What has happened to this great river? What is the source of all this pollution?

Through the years, the Danube has become a convenient dumping ground for growing industry. As the river makes its way to the Black Sea, the wastes of several countries are simply thrown into its waters.

Water pollution comes from nuclear and chemical plants, oil refineries, pulp and paper mills, metal refining and food processing plants, and other industries. Mining iron ore, coal, oil, and gas also produces waste that runs off with water or falls with precipitation. Although there have been some attempts to regulate waste removal and control navigation, enforceable pollution controls hardly exist in this highly populated region.

Half of the drinking water in the Czech Republic and Slovakia, for instance, doesn't even meet the nations' own health standards, and 65 percent of Bulgaria's river water is polluted. Bucharest, Romania's largest city, has no sewage treatment plant at all. Untreated sewage is dumped directly into the Danube. Add to this the

Germans near the city of Ulm enjoy the blue waters of the Danube River (right) as part of a festival. Ulm is less than 100 miles (161 km) from the source of the Danube River.

The Black Sea is polluted by industrial wastewater and runoff from industrial dumps that flows into rivers. Atmospheric pollution, shown here in Copsa Mica, Romania, also settles out on the water or falls with rain.

acid rain that winds bring in from the west, and it is little wonder that the river is in trouble.

In a 1991 article in *Current History* magazine, Stanley J. Kabala wrote, "Austria, Czechoslovakia, Hungary, Yugoslavia, Bulgaria, and Romania join in an assault on the Danube River as it makes its way to the Black Sea. Pollution that begins near Vienna increases so steadily that by the time the river reaches Budapest, swimming in its water is not recommended."

Similar problems face most of the other rivers that flow into the Black Sea. For example, Russia's Kuban River, which empties into the Sea of Azov, is severely polluted by agricultural runoff from the rice-growing region near Krasnodar. It is generally recognized that the water pollution problems in the region are the result of generations of neglect.

Coastal Calamities

Additional pollution enters the Black Sea from human activity along the coastline, including heavy industrial development, increasing populations, and expanding resort areas. All of this leads to additional wastewater, and much of it is dumped—totally untreated—into the sea.

The seriousness of this problem cannot be underestimated. Odessa, Ukraine, with a population of over 1.2 million, dumps most of its wastewater directly into the sea untreated. And none of the towns along Turkey's Black Sea coast even have wastewater treatment facilities.

About 15 million people live in 175 towns along Russia's Black Sea coast. Most do not have wastewater-treatment facilities that are adequate, or many have none at all. Large cities, such as Taganrog, Sochi, Krasnodar, and Rostov, cannot meet water-quality standards because their facilities are old and overloaded. And only 14 percent of the treated wastewater is processed to remove disease-causing organisms called pathogens. The deadly bacteria *E. coli,* which causes stomach and intestinal diseases, is found in high concentrations along populated regions of the entire Black Sea coast.

Along the western shore of the Black Sea, sludge from river dredging is dumped in nearly 20 "official" waste sites. This sludge contains toxic, or

Along coastal areas garbage is sometimes dumped near tourist beaches and hotels. Waste then drifts out to the water or is blown by the wind into the sea.

Dredging keeps channels open, but it can also resuspend sediment that may contain toxic substances.

poisonous, wastes that have settled out of river water. This dumping is causing serious harm to marine life in the Black Sea.

In the late 1980s, 364 drums of toxic waste from Italy were removed from the beaches and coastal areas of Turkey, where they had been dumped. Nobody knows how many more barrels of toxic waste lie in the Black Sea.

Toxic chemicals found in the Black Sea include heavy metals, such as lead, copper, mercury, and zinc. Cyanide and arsenic compounds have also been found. So far, these chemicals have been detected in "safe" amounts. But unless action is taken to stop these pollutants from entering the sea, soon there will be harmful accumulations.

SEA SEDIMENTS

The sediments in the Black Sea provide a rare opportunity to study thousands of years of its ecological history. Each season, changes in sediment deposits are preserved in distinct layers as shown in the picture. The absence of oxygen on the bottom of the Black Sea keeps out animals, so the sediment layers are not disturbed. The sediments are well preserved—they have been stored in the chilly conditions at the bottom of the sea, at about 46 to 48° F (8 to 9 °C).

Studying the sediments of the various layers allows scientists to determine the life forms present in the Black Sea over centuries. Using carbon dating, scientists can learn the approximate age of a layer of sediment.

These sediments enable scientists to tell when plankton biomass was high due to an increase in nutrients. They can detect a rise in the inflow from rivers due to an increase in precipitation in the drainage areas of the rivers surrounding the Black Sea. They can also obtain information about climate, nutrient supply, salinity changes, and pollutants in the sea. Knowledge of what has happened to the sea in the past helps scientists predict what will happen in the future.

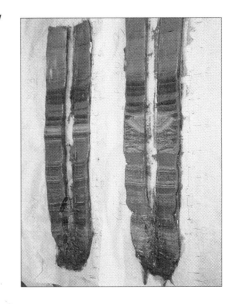

All these toxic chemicals can seriously harm or kill fish. Some damage is already apparent. And people who eat contaminated fish can be poisoned, too. People may suffer damage to the brain, liver, kidneys, and nervous systems—even mental impairment.

Other harmful substances that are found in the Black Sea include organic compounds such as phenol, creosol, and detergents. These come from sewage discharge and the wastes from woodworking, sugar, and other industries. The detergents have caused foamy spots to appear on the sea's surface. But a more serious effect is that many small organisms die when organic compounds disturb the oxygen balance of the water.

Heavy metals and slaughterhouse waste are mixed together as they empty into the Black Sea. Much of this polluted wastewater is stored in open, shallow reservoirs along the Black Sea coast.

Another powerful pollutant in the Black Sea is oil, especially along the coastal regions. In the northwest portion of the sea, where there are several busy ports, there is a film of oil on the water's surface.

Ships frequently travel a route through the Black Sea from the Danube River to the Bosporus Strait. Scientists have also found extremely high levels of hydrocarbons, a sign of oil pollution, along this route. In other areas of the Black Sea where there is less ship traffic the levels are lower. The pollution is believed to be shipping-related.

Many ports along the Black Sea are not properly equipped to handle the heavy shipping traffic and any oil spills that may occur, although Ukraine and Russia have made great strides. The former Soviet military installations and ships that sailed the Black Sea are also sources of oil pollution. Another source may be offshore oil and gas exploration and limited production, which is taking place near the coast of Romania and Bulgaria. So far, there has been no complete or reliable study of the amount or sources of oil pollution in the Black Sea.

Oil can seep into streams and rivers that flow into the Black Sea from poorly-maintained oil refineries (above) located near the coast of the Black Sea.

OFFSHORE OIL AND GAS

Before the breakup of the Soviet Union, Russia supplied its republics and the countries behind the Iron Curtain with cheap oil and natural gas. Since the breakup of the Soviet Empire, however, Russia, now looking for cash, is charging world-market rates for the oil and gas it exports. This has caused hardship for newly

independent countries once dependent on the Soviet Union as a major trading partner. States near the Black Sea are now looking offshore for natural gas and oil in the Black Sea, particularly in the northwest continental shelf region. Ukraine, Romania, Georgia, and Bulgaria are quite aggressive in their search for their "own" energy supplies.

Romania and Bulgaria are already producing some gas and oil. And a British company has recently joined with Ukraine to search for oil. As all this activity increases, so does the possibility for oil spills, leaky pipelines, and oil well blowouts. That probably means more oil pollution for the Black Sea.

Several of these countries, especially Russia and Ukraine, have experience in handling and cleaning up oil spills. Because of their ability to monitor spills by air surveillance and enforce laws that make offenders pay for pollution damage, oil spills along the Russian and Ukrainian Black Sea coastlines almost never occur.

But controlling spills is only part of the problem. Many facilities for unloading and loading oil and gas, such as the one in the picture, are very old and need modernization. Besides updating facilities, most Black Sea countries are going to build new terminals. Russia is expanding its terminals at Tuapse and Novorossisk, Russia's major port on the Black Sea, and probably a new one at Rostov on the Don River. Georgia would like to build terminals at Poti and Batumi. Ukraine will probably build a new terminal to unload oil imports near Odessa. These projects will again add the possibility of more oil spilling into the sea.

The Odessa Declaration adopted in April 1993 requires countries surrounding the Black Sea to produce detailed environmental impact plans before beginning any new projects affecting the Black Sea. But often developing countries need an energy supply and don't have time to comply with any agreement. Some nations are simply disregarding the environmental requirement, or they don't produce a good plan. The result will be a more polluted Black Sea.

Radiation Nightmare

The greatest accidental nuclear disaster in the world occurred less than 300 miles (483 km) away from the Black Sea. An explosion ripped through the Chernobyl nuclear power station in the Soviet Union on April 26, 1986. It was the result of operational errors by engineers testing turbogenerators.

The huge explosion and fire released massive amounts of radioactive material into the environment. Additional danger came from the air contamination carried by the wind. More than 100,000 people were evacuated from the Chernobyl area soon after the disaster. But many people and animals in the path of the wind received serious radiation doses.

Radiation is measured in units called rems. Generally, it is considered safe for a nuclear plant worker to get a radiation dose of five rems over one year. A once-in-a-lifetime dose of 25 rems was

The explosion at Chernobyl destroyed the power plant and poured huge amounts of radiation into the atmosphere.

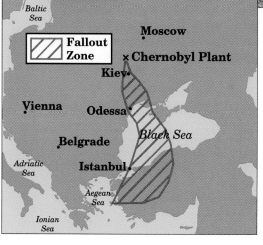

Fallout Zone

Baltic Sea

Moscow

× Chernobyl Plant

Kiev

Vienna

Odessa

Belgrade

Black Sea

Adriatic Sea

Istanbul

Aegean Sea

Ionian Sea

By May 1, 1986, fallout from the explosion at Chernobyl had spread to the Black Sea.

thought to be acceptable for Chernobyl's cleanup workers. But about 24,000 people who were eventually evacuated from Chernobyl received doses of perhaps 45 rems in a very short period of time.

The Black Sea—the closest body of salt water to the site—received a large amount of contamination from the Chernobyl explosion. Additional radioactive material arrived by way of the Danube and Dnieper rivers. Their drainage basins include many of the high fallout areas of Eastern Europe and the accident site itself.

Following the Chernobyl accident, many scientists descended upon the Black Sea region to study the effects of the meltdown. Few other instances of nuclear contamination have been so widely studied.

The good news found by the researchers was that, while levels of radiation in Black Sea fish were higher than normal, they were still within acceptable levels. They believe that radiation levels in Black Sea surface water will return to normal by the year 2000. Even so, some people blame the Chernobyl accident for many of the biological problems in the Black Sea, though they are actually unrelated. Chernobyl has become a scapegoat.

At the Chernobyl site, cleanup is costing billions. Experts decided that the best way to handle the damaged reactor was to entomb it in concrete and steel and leave it alone. Scientists hope to learn about nuclear plant safety from this disaster.

Impact on the Economy

With all the problems the Black Sea region faces—political, economical, and environmental—it will take great effort for people to work together well enough to make a difference. However, by working together, the people of the Black Sea region will ensure a better future for themselves and their children.

The pollution of the Black Sea and inflowing rivers may become an important issue as the region attempts to improve its economy. Pollution can directly affect the economy—for example, the economy will suffer if agricultural products are poisoned by contaminated irrigation water, or if fish populations are destroyed or depleted by pollution in the sea itself.

The resorts on the Crimean Peninsula have been popular with tourists for years. Pollution may spoil this vacation region.

Tourist Troubles

The tourist industry, too, will feel the pinch. It is estimated up to $400 million each year could be lost. The water supplies used by the Crimean Peninsula, which come from the Dnieper River, are said to be extremely contaminated. People living there don't want to drink the water, and tourists are certainly avoiding it.

Waterborne diseases are now increasing. In 1991, for example, a cholera outbreak was reported in Mariupol, Ukraine. Beaches were closed in 1992, and tourism decreased 1,200 percent. It is fairly common for beaches in all other Black Sea countries to be closed temporarily due to unsanitary water conditions.

The fishing boats in the old harbor at Nessebar, Bulgaria are idle. Many Black Sea fishermen have found their livelihoods destroyed because the marine life in the Black Sea has been devastated by pollution and overfishing.

The beauty of the northwestern shelf of the Black Sea has also diminished. The once-blue, sparkling waters are now green and brown. The smell of rot and decay permeates the shoreline. Tourists are beginning to avoid the coasts.

The beaches, a major tourist attraction, are eroding because of reduced river flow. The huge seawalls built to keep the beaches intact are not only ugly but also trap solid waste and floating debris.

Depleted Marine Resources

The Black Sea was once a fertile fishing ground that supported some two million people—primarily the fishermen and their families. With this resource almost gone, the region's economies are in a crisis. Some estimate that over 150,000 jobs have been lost. The Romanian fishing fleet is almost totally out of work.

Two causes for the decline of fishing on the Black Sea are high levels of water pollution and overfishing. Several important fish species, including the bluefin tuna, for example, migrated between the Mediterranean and the Black Sea, but the Bosporus Strait area, through which they swam, has become seriously polluted. Those migrating fish populations are now shrinking rapidly.

Dolphins, too, are rare. Dolphins were once hunted heavily—264,000 were killed in 1954 alone. Measures were finally taken to protect them. The Black Sea Commission placed a 10-year ban on dolphin hunting in 1966, which was extended another 10 years to 1986. Some countries simply chose to ignore the ban, and the dolphin population has not recovered. Scientists are now reporting that "there is hardly a dolphin to be found" in the northern Black Sea. Pollution is probably the major reason this species has not recovered.

Other marine resources have also suffered. Many products, such as raw materials for the various drugs, agar (a gelatinlike material used for thickening foods), and natural dyes, are no longer

OVERFISHING

The decline of fish populations in the Black Sea is also due to overfishing—a result of humans catching fish faster than they can replenish themselves. In recent decades, many fish species have been endangered by the heavy toll fishermen took on their populations.

Turkish citizens have long enjoyed eating fish from the Black Sea (below). Turkey used to rely on the Black Sea for over three-fourths of its fish supply. As late as 1988, Turkish fisheries were going strong, with about 500,000 tons caught in the Sea of Marmara and the Black Sea. But by 1989, that figure was almost cut in half to 264,000 tons. There have been no official figures since 1989, but based on the total tonnage of fish processed at Turkey's largest anochovy plant in Trabzon, most officials think the total catch may have dipped as low as 70,000 tons in 1991.

Turkish anchovies provide one example of the results of overfishing. In 1976, the total Turkish anchovy catch yielded 68,347 tons. By 1984, that amount had increased to 322,758 tons. But suddenly these numbers plummeted drastically. From 1987 to 1989, a total of only 15,000 tons of Turkish anchovies were harvested from the Black Sea.

Why the sudden decline? There are several possibilities. First, the waters were probably overfished. The Turkish government had been supportive of the new technologies that led to greater yields and placed few limits on the size of anchovies that could be harvested. This energetic fishing led to a great decline in the overall anchovy population and its ability to replenish itself.

In addition, Turkish anchovy stock migrates from the northwestern Black Sea where reproduction occurs. This means that the tiny larvae were trying to survive in the very waters where the predatory ctenophore *Mnemiopsis leidyi* is thriving, and most larvae were probably eaten. A possible three to five year moratorium on fishing has been proposed as a way of helping the fish stock recover.

produced because the algae needed to make them no longer lives in the Black Sea.

Native shellfish species, such as clams and oysters, have also been affected by *Mnemiopsis leidyi* and pollution. Some exotic species may turn out to be beneficial, however. Since some species thrive in

There are still many fish markets in the Crimean coastal area, often identified by interesting signs (above).

the low-oxygen, nutrient-enriched conditions of the Black Sea, Bulgarians are working to cultivate an exotic mussel species as a new food resource. Others are looking at a soft-shelled clam species, *Corbula mediterranea*—introduced to the sea in the 1960s—as another food resource. But harvesting shellfish means dredging sediments that are full of toxic wastes. This could resuspend dangerous chemicals in the water and cause additional problems for other marine life.

When fisheries are in trouble because of declining stock, officials monitor the activities of the fishermen to guard against overfishing and make sure enough fish stock is left in the water to replenish the species. Some are suggesting a moratorium on fishing for up to five years to help stock recover. However, in the case of the Black Sea, such measures will not work. They may help in a small way, but the larger problem in the Black Sea is the total collapse of natural environmental conditions. The whole ecology of the sea is changing rapidly, due mainly to land-based activities.

Clearly, humans have caused many problems for the Black Sea. Therefore, it falls on human shoulders to find the solutions. It's not too late—but it's time to get started.

A Romanian health official tests water runoff from a factory for hazardous chemicals.

Chapter Six

Preserving the Black Sea

The Black Sea is a unique region of the world that is threatened and damaged by pollution. But most scientists and government leaders think it is not too late to stop the contamination of the land and water.

If people living in the Black Sea region cooperate and focus on environmental issues, the 1990s should show results from international efforts. There is reason to think the cleanup job can and will be done. But is cooperation in the region too much to ask?

Getting Along

It was quite amazing during the early 1990s to watch the political changes in Central and Eastern Europe. Communism was thrown out of country after country, and even the massive Union of Soviet Socialist Republics fell to the will of the people.

Citizens wanted to rule themselves. They also wanted more open economies and more freedom. People have made great sacrifices to earn their freedom. Often their struggles have created even greater hardships, for new countries usually struggle with inner turmoil. People continue to fight over land, ethnic differences, religion, and politics.

As the old Soviet Empire crumbled, the citizens of Moldova, one of its republics, demonstrated for more freedom.

It has been fascinating to watch history in the making, but environmental issues seem to get lost amid such dramatic events. When people are struggling just to stay alive, worries about saving plankton and reducing phosphate loads don't attract much attention.

The economic situation seems to be slowly improving in many Eastern European countries. Still, with so many problems to deal with in the 1990s, is there time, money, and willingness for the people of these nations to worry about danger to the environment? Ecologists are concerned, because

the entire region is directly affected by the countries surrounding the Black Sea and their use—or misuse—of land and natural resources.

What can be done to stop further pollution in the Black Sea? Can we clean up the Danube? How is it possible to tackle the problems of a river that flows through so many countries and has about 70 million people living along its banks?

A healthy environment does not seem to be in the near future for the Danube. Cleaning up the water will take a great deal of money and time. Western nations will be asked to help. But with the breakup of the Soviet Empire and unrest in many European nations during the early 1990s, restoring the Danube and cleaning up water pollution are not immediate priorities.

Scientists aboard a Turkish research vessel deploy a sediment trap in the Black Sea's deep anoxic waters to obtain samples for study.

Even if nutrients and other pollutants entering the Black Sea were to be somehow reduced right now, the situation would still take many years—and probably decades—to completely reverse itself. The reality is that a reduction in nutrients and pollutants entering the Black Sea will not take place anytime soon. But change has to begin somewhere.

Searching for Solutions

Some citizens of Odessa, Ukraine, look for useable items in the garbage at the open municipal dump (left) located near the Black Sea.

Currently, no single management represents all the coastal countries working to preserve the Black Sea. Such an agency would be very helpful in coordinating research and activities. But credit must be given to the Black Sea countries for taking the first difficult steps toward organization and cleanup.

Government leaders are becoming more concerned about water, land, and air pollution in and around the Black Sea. Pollution problems are discussed at conventions and meetings, and in scientific journals all over the world. The chief weapon in the fight against pollution is information. The

An artifical wetland was created near Varna, Bulgaria, on the Black Sea coast with the help of World Wide Fund for Nature (WWF). Restoring coastal wetlands will provide habitat for animals and help filter out waste in the water.

more people understand about the damage caused by their old practices and the dangers that lie ahead, the more willing they will be to change. The consensus seems to be that the 1990s is the time for change. The damage must stop now.

Efforts to unite governments in the interests of Black Sea ecology have started. A legal Convention for the Protection of the Black Sea, begun in 1985, was signed by all six coastal countries in April 1992. The United Nations Environment Program (UNEP) is helping to create an action plan that will put the agreement into motion.

More recently, the coastal countries appealed to the Global Environment Facility (GEF) to set up a three-year project for "Environmental Management and Protection of the Black Sea." GEF is a $1.4-billion trust fund set up by the World Bank and UNEP to foster worldwide environmental protection. The Black Sea project will help scientists understand the problems, find good solutions, and put emergency plans into action while UNEP's long-term action plan is being developed.

There is a similar project already in place for the Danube River and its delta. Scientists and government officials involved with each project plan to work together to find solutions for pollution throughout the region, since the pollution problems facing the Danube and the Black Sea are so closely

Government attempts to protect the Danube Delta will ensure that Romanian fishermen, shown preparing a dinner of fish broth above, can continue to earn a living in the delta's waters.

linked. Understanding the relationships between the river basin, the Danube Delta, and the Black Sea will enhance all efforts.

In 1992, the GEP began its Danube Delta Biodiversity Project. Since Romania and Ukraine both have portions of the delta within their borders, officials from these countries will participate. Consolidating management efforts in both countries is a priority. Although Ukraine has recently set up a 35,065-acre (15,000-ha) national reserve along the coast, there are too many environmental and research agencies with duplicate responsibilities. And none of them have enough money. The same problem existed in Romania, but conditions are beginning to change. The Biosphere Reserve was organized in 1990 to coordinate management of the delta region. The government also stopped all sand mining and reclamation projects, making conservation its top priority.

Environmental groups in the United States are also involved. Using money provided by the U.S. Agency for International Development (USAID), the Biodiversity Support Program (a consortium of the World Wildlife Fund, the World Resources Institute, and The Nature Conservancy) is helping Bulgaria develop plans to save its endangered wildlife. In another program funded by the U.S. government, a group of universities and environmental organizations are working together to teach business managers from Hungary, Bulgaria, and Romania how to conduct their businesses in the most environmentally sound ways.

The Biodiversity Support Program is working with Eastern European countries to teach people how to take care of the environment. This well-managed municipal wastewater plant in Anapa, Russia, is a model for other Black Sea countries.

Working Together

Another major step toward Black Sea cleanup was taken in April 1991, when the Convention on the Protection of the Black Sea Against Pollution was held in Bucharest, Romania. The idea is that the countries surrounding the Black Sea, working together, can preserve the natural resources of this body of water and protect it from further damage.

The convention established the Commission on the Protection of the Black Sea Against Pollution, with headquarters in Istanbul, Turkey. The commission meets at least once a year to carry out the recommendations adopted by the member nations.

The convention tackled a number of urgent problems. To protect the Black Sea from land-based pollution, it set standards for discharging waste, particularly from industrial and city sewage disposals. It covered ways to avoid oil and other harmful substance pollution. It forbade dumping of all types of radioactive substances and wastes in the area.

Recognizing that the main pollution threat

In 1971, 61 countries met in Ramsar, Iran, for a convention about wetlands of international importance. An agreement was signed that charged each signator to preserve designated wetland areas, called Ramsar sites, in their countries. Bulgaria's four Ramsar sites include the Atanasovsko area of Bulgaria's Black Sea coast (below).

comes from the waters of more than 60 rivers and streams that end up in the Black Sea, the convention vowed to cooperate with the states along the Danube. If the Danube waters are not pollution-free, neither is the Black Sea.

Understanding Causes

Of course, it's most important to understand the causes of a problem before ever trying to work on solutions. Woods Hole Oceanographic Institution in Massachusetts has helped with this by developing a Cooperative Marine Science Program to study the Black Sea.

In September 1991, five ships conducted a research cruise of the Black Sea, gathering information on the sea's physics, biology, and chemistry. Such complete research data had never been collected before. Now scientists planning other Black Sea projects have an excellent database.

There's evidence of more research and education going on. The first classes of the Black Sea

TURKEY TAKES THE LEAD

As one of the most politically stable countries surrounding the Black Sea, Turkey is able to take the lead in cleanup efforts. As far back as the 1970s, Turkish leaders began to take a look at what their country might be doing to the ecology of the Black Sea, including the Sea of Marmara (below). The 1982 constitution actually states that "everyone has the right to live in a healthy and balanced environment." It is now the duty of the Turkish state and citizens to develop and protect the environment and to prevent pollution.

To make sure the environment is protected, Turkey set up several five-year plans. The sixth five-year plan (1990-1994) called for protecting the marine environment and devising a master plan to use the Black Sea coastal areas in a wise and economic manner. Use of chemicals is to be rigidly controlled as are all kinds of waste material coming into the country.

In a speech at a United Nations conference in June 1992, Turkey's Prime Minister Suleyman Demirel said, "Every year Turkey celebrates April 23 as Children's Day. This year, when a primary school-age child took my chair for a while, as is the tradition, the first thing she did was to give instructions for the improvement of the environment. This is only one indication of the increasing public awareness and interest in these issues."

University summer school were held in Costinesti, Romania, from May through October 1993. Experts and scholars were involved in a program to help protect the entire Black Sea Basin. One line of study dealt with the ecology of the Black Sea. The course detailed the slow poisoning of Black Sea waters by suffocating hydrogen sulfide and what must be done to stop the process.

Commitment Needed

It's obvious that awareness of the Black Sea's problems is growing, and governments are willing to begin taking action. Still, long-term commitment remains at the center of the issue. Many cleanup programs now in place are well funded by international organizations. But citizens of the Black Sea region need to see that they can reap more benefits by using good environmental practices than by continuing to exploit the sea.

Though the cost of cleanup is high, the economic and environmental costs of a deteriorated Black Sea would be even higher. The task may seem overwhelming, but it must be done. The Black Sea's history goes back thousands of years. It deserves to have a long and productive future.

Cleaning up the Black Sea will ensure that resorts, such as Clawoia on Romania's coast, will continue to provide jobs and revenue for this developing country.

GLOSSARY

anoxic – water with no dissolved oxygen.

basin – the area surrounding the sea, from which all water drains into the sea.

canal – an artificial waterway used for navigation or drainage.

cilia – hairs used by small marine animals to propel themselves through the water.

ctenophores – small marine animals with transparent, jellylike bodies that use cilia to move through the water.

delta – land built up by deposits of silt at the mouth of a river.

ecology – the relationship between organisms and their environment, or the study of that relationship.

euphotic zone – the surface layer of water through which light can pass.

eutrophication – a process in which the amount of nutrients in a body of water increases, reducing the amount of dissolved oxygen and producing an environment that favors plants over animals.

food chain – the feeding relationships between organisms in which each one eats a lower organism and is eaten by a higher one.

food web – the interrelationship of all the food chains in an ecological community.

macrophytes – marine plants similar to phytoplankton, but which can be seen with the naked eye.

marine – pertaining to the sea.

migration – a mass movement of animals (or people) from one place to another.

nanoplankton – microscopic plant and animal organisms, the smallest of all plankton, which are of very little food value for animals higher up the food chain.

nutrients – chemicals that help living organisms grow.

peninsula – a piece of land jutting out into, and nearly surrounded by, water.

photosynthesis – the process in which plants use sunlight to make their food, and oxygen is released as a by-product.

phytoplankton – microscopic floating plants, especially numerous on the shallow northwestern continental shelf in the Black Sea.

plankton – microscopic plants and animals found in marine environments.

pollution – an addition to an environment that is impure or unclean.

saline – salty.

strait – a narrow passageway connecting larger bodies of water.

FOR MORE INFORMATION

Books

Deming, Susan. *River: A Nature Panorama*. San Francisco: Chronicle, 1991.

Gallant, Roy A. *The Peopling of Planet Earth; Human Population Growth Through the Ages*. New York: Macmillan, 1990.

Hintz, Martin. *Hungary*. Chicago: Childrens Press, 1988.

Kos 'yan, Ruben, editor. *Coastlines of the Black Sea*. New York: American Society of Civil Engineers, 1993.

Murray, J.W., editor. *Black Sea Oceanography*. New York: Pergamon Press, 1991.

Newton, David. E. *Taking a Stand Against Environmental Pollution*. New York: Watts, 1990.

Panighiant, Eugen. *The Danube Delta*. Bucharest: Sport-Tourism Publishing House, 1985.

Parker, Steve. *Pond & River*. New York: Knopf, 1988.

Spencer, William. *Land & People of Turkey*. Philadelphia: Lippincott, 1990.

INDEX

drinking water 42
drugs 51
ducks 33
dumping 38, 42, 44–45, 54, 55
dyes 51

E. coli 44
eagles 32
Eastern Europe 7, 9, 35, 37, 48
ecological balance 34
ecology 25
economy 40, 49
ecosytems 33
electricity 35
energy 30, 47
environmental conditions 52
environmental groups 34
environmental impact plans 47
ermines 33
euphotic zone 39
Europe 5, 16, 20, 32, 33
European white pelicans 33, 34
Europeans 23
eutrophication 38
exotic species 52
explosion 47, 48

fallout 48
farming 12, 34, 37
Ferdinand, King 14
fertilizer 34, 37, 38
fire 47
fish 29, 31, 32, 34, 37, 39, 46, 48, 50, 51, 52
fish eggs 31
fishermen 22, 37, 42, 50
fishing 22, 26, 34, 51, 52
floods 33
fogs 8
food 52
food chain 29, 38, 40
food processing plants 42
food products 38
food web 29, 30, 32, 38, 39
forests 13, 17, 23, 24, 32–33
foxes 32
French 23
fresh water 28, 29, 36, 42

garbage 44
gas 42, 47
geese 33
gelatin 31
Georgia 10, 16, 18, 47
Georgian State Council 18
Germans 12, 18, 21
Germany 10, 12, 14, 18, 21, 25, 26
Golden Fleece 4, 6
Golden Sands Resort 14, 22, 24
Gorbachev, Mikhail 18
government 34

grain 21
Grand Bazaar 8
grasslands 32, 33
grazing 32
Great Britain 23
great white herons 33
Greece 10, 13, 14, 16
groundwater 37
Gulf of Taganrog 18, 31
Gypsy camps 24

habitat 29, 32, 34
hamster 32
harbor 8
Harpies 6
health centers 23
health standards 42
heavy metals 45, 46
Herodotus 7
herring 22
Hitler, Adolf 12
horse mackerel 32
horses 32
Hungary 11, 12, 19, 26, 44
hydrocarbons 46
hydroelectric plants 26, 35, 36
hydroelectricity 26
hydrogen sulfide 28, 29, 36–37

Iliescu, Ion 12
illness 39
industrial development 44
industrial waste 27, 37, 38
industrialization 14, 35, 42
inflow 27, 44, 45
Inguri River 17, 18, 35
insects 33
intestinal diseases 44
invertebrates 29
Iolkos 6
Iran 10, 16
Iraq 16
iron 23
Iron Curtain 47
iron ore 42
irrigation 26, 27, 49
isinglass 31
Islam 16
Istanbul, Turkey 8, 10, 16
Isthmus of Perekop 19, 23
Italy 10, 45
Izmail, Moldova 19

Japan 40
Jason and the Argonauts 4, 6
jellyfish 40
jerboa 32
jobs 50

Kabala, Stanley J. 44
Kakhovka Reservoir 19
Karadeniz 8 *see* Black Sea

Kazakhstan 10, 18
Kerch, Ukraine 19, 21
Kerch Strait 18, 19
kestrel 32
Kherson, Ukraine 19, 26
Kiev, Ukraine 19
Kodori River 17, 18
Kolkhida lowlands 17
Krasnodar, Russia 18, 44
Kremenchug Reservoir 19
Kuban River 18, 44

lakes 33
lark 32
larvae 30
laws 47
lead 45
Lemnos 6
light 39
limestone 23
Lithuania 20
logs 27
Ludwig I 26

Macedonia 6, 10, 14
mackerel 22
macrophytes 39
Main-Danube Canal 10, 21, 26
mammals 32, 33
manganese 17, 21
marine life 25, 29, 45
marine reserves 32
marine resources 50, 52
Mariupol 19, 49
marmot 32
marshes 33, 34
masked polecat 32
Medea, Princess 6
Mediterranean horse mackerel 31
Mediterranean Sea 5, 9, 10, 16, 21, 24, 27, 31
meltdown 20, 48
mercury 45
Mestia, Georgia 17, 18
metals 17, 42
microorganisms 30, 38
Middle Ages 7–8, 17–18
migrating birds 34
migrating fish 51
migration 33, 37
military installations 46
mineral springs 11, 19, 23
minerals 20, 38
minks 33
Mnemiopsis leidyi 40, 51–52
Moldavia 12
Moldova 11, 12, 19
mollusks 30
Moscow, Russia 19
Mount Usba 17, 18
mountain goats 32
mulberry tree 13
municipal water supplies 35
Muscovy 20
mute swans 33
mythology 4

nanoplankton 30, 39
NASA's Coastal Zone Color Scanner 38
national park 17
natural gas 47
navigation 27, 36, 42, 46
Nazi Germany 12
Nessebar, Bulgaria 14, 50
nitrogen 38
North Sea 26
Novorossisk, Russia 18, 21
nuclear reactor plant 20, 48
nutrients 37–38, 45, 52

oak tree 23, 33
oats 19
oceanographers 29, 36
oceans 25, 30
Odessa, Ukraine 19, 20, 22, 27, 44
Odessa Declaration 47
offshore oil and gas 46, 47
oil 21, 41, 42, 46, 47
oil refineries 42, 46
oil spills 41, 46, 47
organic material 30, 38, 39, 46
Osman 16
otters 33
Ottoman Empire 8, 13–14, 16
outflow 27
overfishing 50–51
oxic water 28
oxygen 28, 29, 37–39, 45, 46, 52
oysters 40, 52
Ozal, Prime Minister Turgut 17

paper mills 42
pathogens 44
perch 22
Persian war 7
Persians 17
pesticides 31, 34
phenol 46
Phineus 6
phosphorus 38
photosynthesis 30, 39
phytoplankton 30, 38, 39
pike 22
pipelines 47
plankton 29, 31, 40, 45
plants 28, 30, 32, 34, 36, 38, 39
poisons 35
Poland 12, 19, 20
political upheaval 11
pollutants 37–38, 41, 45, 46
pollution 11, 14, 35, 37, 41, 44, 46, 49, 50, 51, 52
pollution control 41–42
poplar trees 33
population 35, 44
ports 7, 20, 21, 22, 46